The Weakest Among Plants
Gorgeous But Nothing

By

Bernard Benson Sarfo

Also by Bernard Benson Sarfo

The Fact Among Facts (1st)
The Fact Among Facts

Standalone
The Youth Murderer
Be Original Not a Copy
The Christians Science or Scholarship
Precious than Paradise
Habit makes future
A shelter from storm and rain
The Science of Life
The Strongest Lion Knockback
The Perfect and Inspiring City
Above Hope, Faith and Love
The Hero's Brave Decisions
The Weakest Among Plants

Dedication

I dedicate this book to everyone in the world today.

'When wisdom entered into your heart, and knowledge is pleasant unto your soul, discretion shall preserve you, understanding shall keep you' (Proverbs 2:10, 11).

Introduction

Who knows the day of trouble and who can tell the outcome? When shall trouble ceases and the difficulty will be end?

Our way of life has a question and answer that needs to be solved. Who knows what will happen in the next hour?

Who can tell or predict the days ahead and how it shall end? We are like a shadow that goes away without notification. Every human being shall one day drop and will never return again until heavens vanish.

This is sad and unnoticed because we are nothing to boast of ourselves. Oh Lord! Let me learn how I will live in your test and then to have a heart of wisdom and understanding.

Who can continuously watch till the end? When shall noise ceased and the battle will end? What account will you give when you are call to account? How will you discus or explain your case?

Will you be able to answer right? How will life ends you? Will you profit or loss? Who will be your lawyer when you are call to court?

How will you explain your case and what will happen to you at the end? We all have something to discus with the Master and the case to be solved. What will be the outcome?

Contents pages

1. When shall I be call?

What I mine going to answer, when the master calls me? Who will be my lawyer and how is my case will be ending me?

In fact, we have case with the Master and matters that need to be solve. Our history as human beings has a big mark which no balm can heal.

There is a death sentence upon us all as human beings. There is no signal that is prompting us on this matter. No one knows when the death will claim each of us. It always happen unexpected or take us captive unaware.

Our life is at risk each moment with no signals. Oh what a tragedy life! A life, that consists of penalties and death which take us captive without notice. This is serious life that each one needs to be care about it.

There is no second chance or any time again for transformation. When you lose it, you lose forever. Life is precious than gold and silver.

It is peak of all matters that owns everything. There is nothing to compare with life; it is above everything and precious than everything calls precious. Life is short in humans lives due to sin committed by our first parents. We are all at risk and there is no favor at all.

When it turn to you; gone forever. When shall you be called? What will you do? Is there any answer you can give? Oh my dear! We have serious case with the master.

It is appointed for us to die once and after there is judgment which no one can escape. When He calls you, what will you answer? When shall I be call? I do not know, and if I would be call, what will be my reward?

Each one of us needs to think and then behave well; for we have case with the Master. Have you consider yourself well? What do you find? What do you do about it? Is it good or wrong? Will it be well with you, when you are called?

You need to consider your life and then rethink about your deeds. You have case with the Master.

This life is meaningless and there is no profit about it. I mean it does not last as it should be. It is different from what you think for, and different from how you imagine.

It is not fair as you want it to be, and it cannot be as you need it. It varies and cannot be equal. You can imagine but you cannot have it as you wish it.

Oh what a world we live! Sin has damage and crooks everything. Everyone is suffering, whether faithful or not, righteous or not.

What shall we do and what can we do? Oh! This battle is tough and difficult to interpret. In all, what will be your reward? Do you know when you will be call? We do not know when death will claim each one of us.

What we do know is to prepare every day. Do you know when your mouth will close? Do you know when your hands will be bending at your back? We have penalty before us which needs preparation to face it.

Our life is like vapor, which disappears without returns. We cannot know how it will come, but we can prepare when it comes. Our only hope is to take Christ as our personal savior. He is the way; the truth and the life.

Know that, you cannot escape death but you can have life after when believe Jesus Christ dearly. When shall you be call or die?

No one knows, yet prepare and be ready for it. It is appointed for us all. What will be your reward after?

2. What will happen after?

Every tree that is planted bears fruit. So, is the every deed proceeding? Everyone is going to receive his or her reward through the performance revealed. We have rewards with the Master which is equal to the deeds.

What are you going to receive when the Master comes? It is not all when you die, but there is a judgment. Everyone is going to receive his or her price when turns to him or her according to the work done.

Whatever you do, you will be harvested. Great men are not always wise, nor do the aged always understand justice. Do not consider yourself as the mighty, yet be humble and know the time.

But there is a spirit in a man, and the breath of the Almighty that gives him understanding. Whatever the case, everyone is going to face the fruit of his or her deeds. Someone will say or ask, if you die, is it all? Or is there anything again after death?

What do I mean about this content? What will happen after? The Bible has made it clear that there is a judgment after death. If there is judgment, then there will be resurrection. This death that we see is a first death, and also it is a sleep. The time is coming when everyone will be rise from the death.

Those who believe God and accept Jesus Christ as their personal savior will be resurrected when He comes in the second time. Those who did not accept Him would be dead with those who are already dead for thousand years.

When the thousand years are over, Christ will come on this earth again with the saints who had life at His second return with the Holy City (The New Jerusalem) to this earth. Those who did not receive their share at His second return will have their reward after the thousand years.

Here, the fire will come down from Heaven and then consume them. This will be the reward of those who did not have chance to enter Heaven within the second coming of Christ. Here, Christ will pay the wicked according to their deeds by fire and brimstone.

There is a reward for every deeds or work. So, this life is not all, yet there will be reward. What have you considered? Do you respect? What are your deeds? The world will receive it due by it deeds. Do not deceive yourself and never make yourself light whiles you are dark. Do not pretend to be good, whiles you know it is not so. Stop pretending and then do things right and according.

We all have case with the Master. If you look around what do you see? What is going on? What are you doing? What is your share? How do you do your things? This is not all, yet there will be a reward for each deed.

Many people think that there would be no judgment after this life. Others also think that this life is all, there is nothing again. Do not joke of this life and never waste your time on things that are not necessary.

You need to consider yourself well and then do things right. This life is not all, yet there is another thing after this. Do not be wise at your own estimation to destroy yourself. But consider the outcome and then behave well.

This life is not all, yet there is judgment which nothing can be compared. My dear, we have case with the Master, so know how to behave and then do things according to the requirements. There is judgment and reward after this life.

3. Will this be good results?

You shall receive the reward according or equal to work done. Every farmer harvest fruit of the tree he or she planted. So, your deeds will determine your results. It depends on your deeds or your acts that you always do.

This life has lot to face and a lot to demand. Whatever we exhibit determines the outcome and then makes the reward. Your achievement resulted by your work done. So, also your reward confirms your achievement.

What results do you want to achieve? How did you live? What have you considered? How did you go about? Our actions determine the life we will live and then set the goals ahead of us. What have you done?

What do you want to achieve? There are many things ahead of us but what will these things will lead us to? Have you consider those things and how have you determine to go with? Is there anything that entices you?

What is your interest? How did you live your life? Oh! Who will save me from all these troubles? This life is hard for me and I cannot go without (You) oh God! Will this be your word? If you accept your condition, and then consider God, your life will be worthy. Do not let the world lead you. Never accept to live a cheap life, yet value your being and then live faithful. Do not go with smart people, but go with God fearful men and obtain wisdom.

Do not take the world and then leave God, yet consider God first and then live your life. Why die before your time? Though things are fighting against you both spiritual and physical, yet hold your dignity to the end.

Do not throw yourself down because of poverty. Never abuse yourself due to force of the earth. Always know that, there is a reward for every deed. You need to consider every little thing and then value it. For you do not know what your dream will end.

Fight the good fight of faith and then hold the truth to end. Do not force yourself to do things that are contrary to the laws of nature. But consider the outcome and then keep yourself well. If you keep this in mind, then you will be safe.

The world has teachers that teach every day lessons of life, but what will those lessons will lead you to? This comes in the content, will this be good results? If it will be, it depends on the acts been exhibited. Do not take things for granted, and never go where you are not allowed to go. Know how to walk; know how to talk, know how to dress and prevent short comings.

For all these things will be bringing into judgment. So, it is your turn to proof yourself as a faithful man. Do you have a lawyer? Will your lawyer will be able to save you? If it is so, then it depends on your ability that you proof in life.

Do not disturb yourself about the world goods, neither wish things as without law. But live a life without a question mark. As it stands on you, do your best to glorify God. Be faithful like Job; stand boldly as Daniel, and then live like Noah.

These people are faithful and God is pride about their life and their integrity. Will this be good results? Yes, if we stay in as we have been taught.

This life is not all, yet there is a judgment after. But time is not known by anyone. I wish you well, but be considerate in all things. Will this be good results? It will be determine by your doings and faith in Christ.

4. Who knows the evil hour?

As the sleep come without notification, so evil hour comes without sound of awareness. It comes as a thief in the night with no notice. A life cannot be certain without hope and there nothing that grow without nursing.

The world has so many things but good life depend on principles. Who can tell good or bad times ahead of us? Whatever the life will be; there is hope, unless we disregard it. Do not show yourself as you know everything, yet be considerate and learn other things from humility.

Do not raise your shoulders, because of your power. Do not walk over others for your strength sake. How can tree grow without rain, means without God you are nothing. It seems you are great in your own eyes.

A little child can teach you a lesson. Many leaders sometimes disregard their servants; yet some of them do not know that, without their servants, they are not leaders.

There are stages in life and also lessons that needs to be study at each stage. Without humility, these lessons cannot be known. Means you cannot bear any fruit without humility. You need to come down, for where you are standing is too high.

When will you come down from where you are standing? You can turn to everywhere you like; but know that, there is a reward for each deed.

Who knows the evil hour? It seems you are giant and strong and you do not fear anything? You have not seen what you should see? And you haven't heard what you must hear. Yet know that, there is accountability.

Who knows the evil hour? Do not be wise at your own estimation and never abuse yourself through bribe. But fear God and eschew evil. Who knows the evil day? Do not oppress others who are weak and never step on the servant due to your wealth.

Know that you shall reap whatever you will sow. No one knows the evil day and no one can tell the outcome or the results; so be considerate and set yourself apart. Whatever the life has the profit, whether good or bad.

Everyone will face the realities of life matters, it does not matter your beauty; wealth and strength. Know that, there will be an evil day. Can you escape? Be considerate and then open your eyes well and then watch. Watch out! There is a word coming that no one can explain it.

Know that you can meet a case without your knowledge. Be careful and then watch your steps; your mouth and your actions well.

Do not disturb yourself in the world, yet know how you will live in. do not pick things on your chest yet pick them one after another.

But know the best and pick that one. Who knows the evil hour? Do not leave your home without preparation, yet put things together and leave.

Means try and do things right through plan and preparation to fulfill your purpose in life. Be ready always and set your goal right for the benefit of you and others. Do not throw your dignity aside but make sure you are on the line.

Prepare yourself and set your time well to prevent late in this evil days. Be considerate always and live upright.

In fact, many people joke of life and regardless of its penalties. Others do not mind what will come; in fact they do not know how serious the results will be.

Everyone must learn how to be ready for any life regardless the season. That is, we must be ready to respond any call that will come, because we cannot escape death and judgment. Who knows the evil day?

5. How will this be?

No one knows how this will be and reward attach to it. But what you should know is to prepare yourself for any outcome. Consider the little things and plan to practice good deeds. In all; what will you harvest?

Where will be your stand? Will you gain justice? How is your life? This is great and that is difficult to understand. When shall you repent from your wrong doing? Will you continue in doing wrong or right? How long will you correct your mistakes?

In fact, no one knows the degree of punishment God will impose on the wicked. How will this world would be look like at the end of this world? Who can interpret it? We have case with the Master. What will be your response to the Master?

Do not take the world into your bosom. Never set your time above the normal. Do not exalt yourself more than the limit, but consider the punishment and make your move on the right order.

How will this be? Is my life on it way? What I mine doing to myself? How long will I stop deceiving others? Shall I continue cheating others? How will this be? How long shall I consider myself on these matters?

When shall I cease murdering others with my mouth? Could this be good end? Will this be well? When will you consider your actions? Do not put yourself into trouble while there is no trouble.

How will this be? In fact, there will be a time when all things will come to an end. Everyone will one day receive his or her reward according to the deeds exhibit. So, do your best to prevent wreck and then solve problems.

Do not exalt yourself yet, come down and then prevent damage. Will what you be reward? Will it be happy; good or bad? How are you going to be rewarded? The people in the world will one day going to account for the deeds they exhibited.

Everyone will be pay according to work done. Let everyone consider his or her deeds to suit the occasion. Your actions will receive reward suited. Do not measure your work with your strength but measure it with your attitude to determine the outcome.

How will this be? Means every work or deeds will be measured by heart been used. The reward will show the heart that was used for the work done.

Do not deceive yourself; neither deceives others, because no one will carry your burden for you. The time will tell and the hour will be determining the crown which you will receive. Be faithful and then hold your integrity to the end.

Do not appear as a light without good deeds. Yet accept your condition and then make change. How will this be? When will this end? And what will be your reward? Do not receive applaud from the men through deception of your deeds.

Do not force yourself to do things in deceitfulness. Yet do your honest part according to your strength to prevent ruin of your soul at the end. This message is too hard for me, will you do? It is a message for a man.

Hold it and do your part as a faithful servant who has done his honest part. How will this be? What will be your reward? What penalty will you face? What will be your lot? Who will be your help? What answer will you give when you are asked?

My dear brother or sister, this world will not last forever and you too cannot last any longer, because of the sin penalty caused by our first parents. So, it is time to repent from all your wrong doings. How will this be? Note:

6. Is there any hope?

Yes! It is not all lost, yet there is hope for each one of us. Unless you do not accept it or do not consider it's important. Life is precious than anything and it is wealth that everyone has.

Without it, there is no world or any other thing. Though, things are not in order as it should or must be. But it is not without hope. It is not late at all, if you are alive. But you cannot be wealth unless you live according to the principles of life.

Precious things deserve precious life but peak of all life is to fear God and eschew from evil. Why do you want to destroy your life? Why have you make things just like that, as there is no judgment.

Do not throw yourself on the ground, neither misuse your time; yet be considerate and live well. Do not kill yourself because of your poverty, neither disregard your time as of no use.

There is time for everything and future for great expectation. It shall be well do not give up or dismay. Take note of every step you make and consider every hour of your doings. Make use of every second's and let every minute produce precious life and good behavior.

Do not live as the world move; neither mix of them, yet be a light among them, may be you will save one of them as your crown. There is hope for everyone who has life, it is not late yet.

It is seems there is no other time and there no other chance. Do not think so, you shall have your share. Do not give up or dishearten. It shall be well. Oh! When will these things pass away for me to have rest for my soul?

It is enough, I am tired, and I cannot go further. Why me? Things are not moving well and it is sad to talk of it. People are laughing at me, yet others shout on me. What must I do? Where from all these?

Whatever you see, will not last, it is a temporal not permanent. There is hope for your time but the time is not known.

It is unknown time but look forward for it and be hopeful. It is not late; it shall be well. Be patient and wait to the due time set by God. It is not late at all; wait and keep watching. You shall see the King in His glory and power that fulfill all questions and answers.

The troubles of this world shall end and the things that are disabling shall be fully restore.

The things shall pass away and the new ones shall be restore by God. The heaven and earth will be renewed and all the host of them will be renew. There is hope, this life that is fill of troubles will be forever end.

Those who have prepared shall meet the King in the air. He is coming with the clouds and all eyes shall see Him.

Our hope is to trust God and have confidence in Him. This troubles that you see today shall come to pass.

Do not disturb yourself of the world matters, neither put your trust in it, it does not last. Be strong and be of good courage, yet these things will end eternally.

Is there any hope? Yes! There is hope in future and the good end for those who trust God. What have you considered? What are you doing? What is it about your life? How do you live? Your hope will be determined by your actions today. But there is hope for everyone who believes.

7. What will be your reward?

Good and excellent work receives excellent wealth and renowned recognition. The highest receives dear name and glory. But the bragging mouth profits nothing. It is you who deserve that applaud and fame.

But what good job have you done? What is that work you have done? Good deeds receive good reward, and bad deeds also receive bad reward. So, your work will determine your price. When shall you repent from wrong doings?

The trees that bear fruits sustain the eater and the one who work deserve to eat from the work he has done. Profit comes by production but the amount of wealth determine by the volume of the product. This means that, your reward will be determined by your production.

What production have you made? What is your work? How do you do it? What is your attitude towards your work? What difference have you made in your work? Do you cheat in your work?

Are you faithful in the little that you have? When will you cease from lying? Do you pay your workers the right price they deserve? What are you doing? Is it right or wrong? There is a reward for every deed and the price for every product. What you will have; will be what you have worked for. Whatever you will sow; you shall reap it. It is all that it will be count for you, but what you have work for; that you shall receive.

So, the reward will be equal deeds or the work you did. In fact, whatever we intend and will comes true in our lives. The reward will be your choice and the fruit you plant for. Our action witnesses the thoughts and move makes it clear.

This world will pass away but those who consider God will live. It is abundant for you to know God and it is opportunity for you to find out more things that concerns life. Do not stop search out for God the Heaven and earth Creator.

It is your duty to know Him than anything that He has created. It is your benefit to do more about your life for sake of your future position. Do not wait for miracle before doing something about your life.

It stands on you to do something concerning your future reward. Many people work for food instead of life; others search for weeds instead of food that will sustain their life. Means many people do not have right purpose for their future. But live any way and anyhow. That is, they disregard the purpose by which they created for and then live madly on behalf of selfish life. Others promote vanity instead of meaningful life.

Oh what a tragedy! Where are you focusing and what do you want to reap? Do you have aim? What is that aim? Where will this aim lead you to? Will it be the needed one which the Master is looking for?

Due that aim suits the reward? Whatever you will do will determine your share at the end. God will bring everything into judgment whether good or bad. When shall you repent from your wrong doings? What do you want to do to yourself?

Why damaging yourself with unnecessary things? When shall you do things well? What do you want to have? What cloth do you want to wear? What appearance do you want to go with?

Do you want to shout doors of the opportunities? Why are you disturbing your life? What crown do you want to have? Do not let the world bought your mind and neither lead by the world. You will be paid according to your work. Do not deceive yourself and never make yourself light whiles you know you are dark. But in all, God will have on you if consider Him and then come to Him.

The time is not known or the day of evil is not known by anyone. In fact, no one knows when he or she shall be calling by death. But there is hope for each one of us.

Let us all consider our ways and doings and then eschew from evil doings. For God bring everything into judgment whether good or bad. You must note it, and keep yourself pure. May God bless you and your works! Be hopeful and then consider your ways and actions.

8. Beautiful for Nothing Flower

Adam was more privileged than his children. It was possible for him, the first father, to have life eternal than his followers but he prevented it.

Today, we are in a situation where everlasting life has departed from us forever but people in this world struggle for all the world's goods. Selfishness has taken over our state; we chase the world and its goods, which can never give eternal life.

Our condition as human beings is in the state which cannot escape death. You can add up to your body – but you cannot add up to your life. You can add to your life through Christ.

Food is profitable to the body but when the body dies, food is no more beneficial to it. You can fill your body with food but you cannot add anything to your life. Why then do you want to fill your body with food, which is temporary?

You cannot pick everything for yourself, when you know it is going to be a waste. And you cannot also waste everything. Appreciate the little you have and let others also get some. Because you will be a waste, allow others. Let others have it. You cannot take all for yourself. Beautiful flower, but there for nothing! Beautiful flower, but not lasting! Beautiful flower, but there for a moment!

You are no more, even when you are living. And you cannot be anything, when you die. You are there as a stream without source but a flood of rain only for a moment.

Why are you taking all of what is there for all of us? Beautiful but momentary, beautiful but profiting nothing to the world! A human being will be a waste, so don't stress your-self to get everything.

Our situation is not as profitable as expected; that is, God created us to be more than we currently are. Our condition is with hope and without hope.

That is, sin has become our decision maker, and it decides our destiny. We should not waste what is left for us. Some people are so selfish that they want everything in this world for themselves only. That should not be the case.

You can become a hero on earth but zero in heaven. Why are you taking all for yourself? We are in a situation whereby we can die at any moment. Due to this situation, we must be careful of whatever we are doing. We must be watchful.

9. Considering Bad Times Whilst Enjoying Good Times

Humans, sometimes, forget themselves and fail to consider their condition – death – which has come to stay until the second coming of Christ. Enjoy life but consider bad times.

Our nature does not last as it should be. We forget our being, when life goes on well. We always forget our condition as dead beings.

Good times are characterized by happy moments, and happy moments cause you to forget the bad times ahead of you.

When things go on well in life, we even forget God, who created us. We always enjoy life, when things go well. When humans become rich, we even forget to seek help from God.

Enjoyment of life can cause damage to the mind and reason as well. Good life worries less of things around its environment.

That is, it does not fret over those around. Enjoying good life may give room to pride, if care is not taken. People forget themselves when they have fun. Sometimes, when you have money to purchase anything you want, you don't care how much it costs because you have more money.

It is important to consider bad times too. When you have money, sometimes, you don't mind what is coming. You, sometimes, do things the way you want, whether it's good or bad.

It is interesting that, when some people get money, they don't respect again. Pride takes the position of their being, and they, sometimes, speak harsh words to those around them.

Those who have not experienced bitterness in life pride themselves in what they have; they forget that dark days may be ahead of them.

Nobody in this world will get the opportunity of enjoying only 'good days' in his or her life without encountering any seeming misfortune.

Life cannot be fair only, so we need to consider the things we do in this world. Life is mixed with good and bad experiences. All things can be ours but all things cannot be yours only; we are in a world of inter-dependence. It is not good enough to enjoy life all alone without helping others who do not have.

Consider when you have what you need and be mindful of how you handle it, because nobody knows which day is a disaster?

Enjoy life as you have but consider your movement, because this world cannot be yours forever.

Be mindful of all your doings; your life must be beneficial to others. Refresh others and others will refresh you. Be humble, lest you stumble and crumble and lose hope.

10. Living as If All Things against You

Sometimes, life is as if you were dead but still alive. It, sometimes, becomes dark unexpectedly. Other times too, it appears that you are not part of life; you feel as if all people have rejected you.

It becomes unbearable and difficult to live. You feel lonely, whether you have a husband, a wife, children or friends. Life, sometimes, becomes bitter than the term 'bitterness'.

In life, sometimes, light becomes darkness for you, and you wouldn't know what to do or where to go. Sometimes, you feel dead even though you are still living; life seems hopeless to you.

Life becomes very difficult; people live on survival skills. Happiness becomes sorrow and mourning.

In times like these, never let hardship put you down or discourage you. Every man or woman born into this world is already victorious because of the opportunity to live.

God has given us the chance to know him, who created heaven and earth. And this opportunity is your reward for you to know who God is.

Sometimes, circumstances in life which you think are your end are a tool for your victory and to help draw you closer to God.

Never think of loss because of the poor situation you find yourself in. The condition is there for only a moment; it will not be there to the end of your lifespan.

Never be discouraged, because of the hardship you are going through. Exercise faith in God and be hopeful till the end.

Hard times are opportunity days to discover your real being and your destiny. Never doubt God because of hard times. In life, hard times teach us lessons of bitterness and the carefulness we should know for our progress.

We must accept every condition we are in and manage it well. Never announce your condition or make noise of your situation. All our conditions are aspects of our life's progress and benefits in every situation. In this world, every life has its record and reward.

The lives we live cannot be equal; so are the situations that we are passing through. Every life has its unique ways and conditions that one must pass through.

Never think that you are cursed because of the hardship you are going through. Sometimes, life becomes unbearable but do not think it is a curse.

You may even prefer dying to living. That is, you dislike existence in its entirety. But never kill yourself; look up to God for a breakthrough, and good things will happen to you.

Bad days are like taking bitter drugs, but bitter drugs too are remedies for some bad situations.

It is evident that bad days also produce good results and bring out new ideas. '

All things work together for good to those who love God' (Romans. 8 Verse 28). So never give up on bad days. God has thousands of ways to provide for you. Never be discouraged, for your possession is available to claim; take it.

11. Life's Carefulness and Profit

Life can be sweet by carefulness and determination. And proper attention is the key that reveals knowledge and understanding.

Carefulness brings good wealth and gives profit even to the foolish. Having a fresh thing with a fresh mind is better than an old thing used by an unknown person.

A new experience brings new knowledge; new knowledge brings research; and research brings broad knowledge and understanding. A fresh husband is better than an old husband who wants to become fresh.

In life, some people want to get everything on a silver platter rather than use accepted laws and regulations. So many people take things for granted.

Taking precautions prevents accident, and it helps to rightly do things. Some people don't think before they act; rather, they act before they think.

Almost always, we make mistakes in the things we do. Sometimes, we do things hastily without considering what the outcome would be.

We always pack up before thinking. But profit comes by carefulness of doing things. Never fail to plan; if you do, you have planned to fail.

12. The Proud Acts

The worse of life ever practice and the most disadvantage behavior that causes the doom of life; is think of self-beauty or being proud of one's self in the manner of self-important or agreeable yourself than the other.

These acts revolve on ladies (women). The practice of competition among women is higher than men. And the manner, in which it is practice, has caused damage to all people in the world.

Women weakness has damaged the world beauty in terms of correct life management. Women always feel proud and wish the acts of flesh than the spiritual.

The girls have picked these acts and want to live by sentiment. There is nothing so dangerous than to feel proud of yourself and behave by your emotion.

Girls sometimes act as if they are on top of everyone. Ladies who enter university level, some regardless of their colleagues who haven't. Some women feel proud of their beauty and wants to take advantage of everything concerns life.

Today's young girls have taken the illegal track and attitude contrary to life principles and are doing what they like. They have taken their shoulders up and behave like birds fighting on food.

That is, they are always ready to promote evil acts and ready to stand for their right to do that. Girls always want to challenge themselves and act as if no one is like them; they feel pompous and want to show off.

You cannot stand well whiles you are on the muddy area. That is, you can't have a good atmosphere by your negative attitude and you cannot push without position yourself well.

Means every act in life comes by intent and the result makes the difference. They must be honest and prudent in order to have a remarkable name and praiseworthy; which is valuable and admire by people.

In fact, life is not a fashion. But it is principles and the fate matter. Young ladies must have patient about life and move wisely. They are to take note of every step they make and fixed their steps well.

Girls must be alert about their life and manage it well. All acts have what it takes about life and nothing can be done well without good attention. Your misused life today is the penalty at your future scandal.

Never abuse your life by sexual immorality or other things else and lose your wealth. You can lose your gold because of your acts and dismantle your life diamond hardly to repair or refine as you wish at first. That is, you cannot have your quality life again if you lose it.

You must consider everything you do and beware of the shoes you ware. That is, be careful about in and out actions and manners. You must build your life with a good attitude and special ingredients for your beautiful praise.

Proverbs 14:1- 4

Says;

The wise woman builds her house, but with her own hands the foolish one tears hers down.

2 Whoever fears the Lord walks uprightly, but those who despise him are devious in their ways.

3 A fool's mouth lashes out with pride, but the lips of the wise protect them.

4 Where there are no oxen, the manger is empty, but from the strength of an ox come abundant harvests.

The effort introduces in everything, erect good or bad fruit but carefulness in doing brings the welcome atmosphere and results in peace life. If you want yourself good, good will come, equally the bad ends the same.

Young women must be careful about in and out actions and make the prudent decision for themselves and never lose the opportunity they have, else they will go through tremors they will never forget.

They must live carefully and watch their acts towards everything they do. Life is not like quiet sleep or resting in the guest house, but it is a continuous fight, that needs not rest or stop. One mistake causes much trouble and destroys life ability and brings life penalties.

Currently, ladies have made the world so dirty and have destroyed correct thinking because of their attitude in dress, and they never mind the consequence. In fact, the world today is for the women and the women are for the world!

Everything in the world is now moving by the women and the world has damage through the manner of their appearance.

This is true and there is no doubt about it and many of them witness and even make comments on that. It is their news and it bears evidence against them!

If adult women will change their style of living and make a good example as prudent women, the young girls will make the world beauty as rosy and the world will take its healthy cloth again. Following the world beauty is nothing but the fear of God makes a difference.

Note this scripture;

Proverbs 31:30, 31

Charm is deceptive, and beauty is fleeting, but a woman who fears the Lord is to be praised.31 Honour her for all that her hands have done, and let her works bring her praise at the city gate.

The acts shown today by many young girls are horrible and it needs attention. The manner in which some of them behave is unacceptable. When life takes bad root it goes beyond the margin, and it is difficult to dig for the end. But many of them entertain it.

In fact, women are far advance in negative attitudes than men and it is obvious. They know how to hide sin than digging or searching for gold.

Obviously, women can control the men by their acts and dismantle the good name ever known. If the women take off their negative hat, the sun of rain will forever cease and the world we live today will be light of happiness.

What am I want to say; the world we live today can be fair and the best place to stay depends on the style of the women willing to live.

The attitude of many young girls has deformed many of the boys today. In fact, when it comes to the character as we all knew that makes a person.

Many women do not care about their acts or never mind to show the negative side of it, to disturb their colleagues and are ready even to do more to make it worse. This is true, they mean to sin than to spare.

Further, women are pretenders or want to show off or pretend to be good-looking. Women are very pretenders and have deceived acts than men. Many women acts are deceptions and always want to defend their false acts.

The world we live in has a lot of lessons and notes to be considered. This world cannot cover it beauty again till Christ comes and there is no other chance that can be entertaining for the best life.

But if care is taking, we will benefit some positive lifestyle. The only thing we can do is to be careful about the way we live and take note about every step we make. The Lord is coming!

Many acts are destroying our being every day and night that result in eternal death but the women always entertain it.

In fact, if women will decide to live a positive life, this world will somehow turn a bit positive atmosphere and the storms that always take men will semi- cease.

However, life lessons are notes to correct the wrong acts but if we neglect the experience that resulted, then, we cannot cover it again as we wish. Misuse life has nothing to cover again in the best state as a wish but the life well manage can have what it takes.

Many girls put their life into a second fiddle and wish to act fleshly. They think that everything is normal and considered not. Eating as they wish and walk as they like; cloth anyhow and never listen to the advice or take note of the life matters.

Women can change the world; if they consider the life principles and live according to the laws governing life acts, and then nothing will be needed again for best life traffic.

If the women will manage life according to its best and take care of their acts, then men will cease from mind murdering and have their being as a whole. Women must consider their acts and live modestly.

Note this scripture:

First Peter 3:1-5

Wives, in the same way, submit yourselves to your own husbands so that, if any of them do not believe the word, they may be won over without words by the behavior of their wives,

2 when they see the purity and reverence of your lives. 3 Your beauty should not come from outward adornments, such as elaborate hairstyles and the wearing of gold jewelry or fine clothes.

4 Rather, it should be that of your inner self, the unfading beauty of a gentle and quiet spirit, which is of great worth in God's sight.

5 For this is the way the holy women of the past who put their hope in God used to adorn themselves. They submitted themselves to their own husbands.

There is nothing short in nature, which needs to be modified or refine in another way for the best use. The things created were perfect from the beginning and well please.

But suddenly something strange happened and things created lose the exact state of its nature. Every act has the effect and can be resulted negatively or positively at the end. One mistake can create damage without remedy and can earn in eternal lose.

Women must be carefully considering their actions in any manner of life and they must watch out their dress wearing currently.

The miserable state of the world today stands on the manner of the women clothes themselves and the stylish of it nature appear in public causing mind disease and blocking correct nature of thinking, increasing lust of the eye and resulted in shamefulness.

There is nothing so dangerous than making yourself stumbling block for others or plan to make people fall by your appearance by pretending.

At the moment, women purposely appear in the manner that causes mental or spiritual fall, to destroy correct thinking and to set trap for people to lose their life.

Women today have totally decided their stand in dressing and showing the side which they are and decide their eternal home by the manner of their cloth; never put me wrong; I am telling you the truth.

Every dress wear represents the character and the manner of your appearance shows what you have decided. Many people do not know what they are about in life and what they are doing about life, taking things for granted and behaving as they wish.

Most of the women are so serious to act negatively and never mind to create what will cause harm to other people's lives and many of them are happy in doing that.

Your act can decide your destiny and can make a negative or positive home for you. All things done on earth have the peak or low estimate which can complete or incomplete of the project of life been set up.

Women love eyes beauty than inner beauty and promote weeds than the seed. That is, they loved what will destroy a few days than what will last long or wish moment than hours or days.

They love food ready to eat, than the food preparing to eat, that is, they want things fast than waiting before the best time and that is their lot that is why we are all suffering today.

Women are the keys and the men are the doors, women can lock and open men in all matters of life and men have no say.

Women have access to life avenues, and they are welcome everywhere in the world because they have the key of access, but they never know because of lack of self-actualization and they lack considering about life issues.

They weigh all things light and considered not the outcome. Women lack the spirit of forgiveness and they are also ready to curse than to bless when they are offended.

They lack patience in life but ready to provoke than to make happiness. Many of them are very lazy and not willing to work from the heart.

They are gossip and active in making fun of others and to pull down others dignity. All these acts deform their beauty and closed their insight for earning the best life at the end.

Many of them lack understanding and difficult to accept their fault. But women have control, because of their attractive form. And if care is taking, they can turn the world around in its better state and the world will be partially nice.

As the strong wind sometimes throw out dust to the eyes of the people, so to the women who intentionally dress negatively makes dust around the globe for to hurt many eyes and to destroy the correct thinking with their acts.

Women must take care of how they act in all manners of life. I wonder why women love the world and its goods that benefit nothing and always hoard up belongings.

In fact, this world cannot and will not give anything worthy and help otherwise. But if women will be vigilant and decide what is right about life, then the world will shire and favor all of us and life will be fair. This message needs your consideration!

13. The Unlikely Age acts

The world has a lot of notes and many incidents difficult to understand. There are things going on marvelously in the sight of man today seriously aggressive in the things ever happen before.

Young boys and girls are very vanity at their stage in terms of acts that always going on their life. Their age has no competition in life and because of their dependency; most of them don't think about what will happen tomorrow.

They live as they wish without attention. But life results depend on this stage whether good or bad. If there are stages in life which must be carefully considered; it is the young stage.

Children must be taught and train as well and monitored all the time. Their stage needs much attention by their parents and considers their act at each moment. The children do not consider life matters but act from pressure and wish.

They need to be directed by their parents every time. Many parents fail on how they should monitor their children but they only think about what they will eat and dress and leave the rest that matters.

That is, their conducts are out of counting by their parents but this shouldn't be. The basic acts of children are the penalty of their future goal and the harvest is managed by the grounds promoted or sowed. They should behave well and think of the result.

Children are like stream form by the raining water that does not have direction and can be lost at each time the rain ceased. That is, they do not have any stand when it comes to life as it should be live.

They need support and guide to survive by their parents. Correct Life management starts with the correct management in the childhood stage by their parents' guide and the fruit that bears depends on the act managed at their stage by their parents.

Children must be cared seriously by their parents and support as well. In fact, life results mostly stand on the acts in the childhood stage and as the results of this, parents must be very close to their children at the age of three to ten years.

This age holds the deeper form of acts resulted in good or bad in the future of their children. Children do not think but behave to show their thinking.

That is why the child is known by their acts. And this is a fact without doubt if care is not taking concerning their acts at their stage, and then forms their destiny without knowing by their parents.

Parents must consider their children live acts in all the time and take note of their doings each and every day and guide them of their doings.

One of the reasons why children are vanity stands on their acts and they are thoughtless of whatever they are doing.

Their life cannot be managed by themselves except it guide by the mature person and those who have experienced life in the circumstance. The children must be guided by the way they should go, so that, at their age, they can cope with every situation.

Note the scripture:

Proverbs 22: 1, 6, 15

A good name is more desirable than great riches; to be esteemed is better than silver or gold.

Start a youth out on his way; even when he grows old he will not depart from it.

Folly is bound up in the heart of a child, but the rod of discipline will drive it far away.

The children must be guided and teach. They lack the total choice of the idea but ready always to receive any acts impose on them. They are ready by any life wind blow on them and lack the choice of right from wrong.

The youth are subjected to negativity. They always make foolish things and are subject to any pressure, and have no choice. That is, they take whatever flashes in their sight and behave any manner of life set before them.

Your child acts today will be the name of his or her destiny. Parents are responsible for their children's acts and the manner they live in. The children are like the mountain, they receive and respond to any sound heard.

So, it is the parent's duty to guide and to protect their children from any act or danger which can result their life ruin in the future.

14. The Knowledge Acts

Life experience is about understanding in life matters and the responds of that life shows the maturity stage. The things done on earth have a way of doing. And there are lessons involved in the move. There comes experience. The masters' key.

Life has stages. Through these stages there experience grows and act according. Life without experience is immature and fruitless.

The experience acts are the life fruit that one has to do correct things and to apply for the benefit of others. That is, that person knows what to do and understand the results.

The experienced act is the best way to handle things in a matured way and the best way of doing things. When one has experienced in life, his or her management in life is secure and fearless.

Experienced produce care and the care produce security and understanding. The one who has experienced in daily life activities have a balance in life management and produce good result about life issues.

In fact, those people live without fear and make a prudent decision about whatever comes in life. Mistakes in life are the teachers that teach lessons of care which prevent the eternal damage of life and prompt us on the things without our knowledge to be well aware off.

In life, the weakest man with mature experience can live at least a better life with well balance acts. But not all can manage life with the experienced gain. It depends on the attitude of an individual who knows the laws of life and how it was managed by circumstance encountered.

Many people have a lot of experience in life but not all can manage the trials in life and live upright. Experience teaches lessons of patience and in the practical way of doing things as well.

In life, the experience makes the difference in capacity of the performances or responds to the mature acts, well known of individual who can manage than the other. And without experience, things cannot be managed well. Means managers must be knowledgeable and practically know where to start life again when things go wrong.

Everyone needs to have some amount of experience in life; else life cannot be managed as well. In fact, every human being needs to have a skill which is the life food to survive and to have his or her being up to the point needed in the life journey.

The nature of our being was designed for activities. The members of our being function by exercise, and through this activities knowledge is gain; and there comes the experience, which is the life wealth that protects us from enemies that destroys courage.

Note that, lack of experience brings a lack of competency. And the manner of that life becomes objection.

Our life stages show how we should be patient, and manage the life step by step as the day goes. Life is managed in days, not a moment. And it needs stages in order to progress, and that is how God created us to live and have the need at every stage which is equal to the age and manages it well.

That is why hours, days and years are given to us to know what it means to have the best in life than ruin our life. Those who want things quick destroy their life and lack wisdom and knowledge about life.

However, life in this world concerns bitter, good, bad, happiness as the results of sin. But for us to manage life as to the wish, depends on experienced gain.

Life lessons bring development and bear the fruit of patient that represent total understanding. In life, the patient carries the key to success and opens fortunes at the right time.

But the one who lacks experience in life can damage handover property and discourage by trials. But the one who holds the courage through life experience withstands every trial.

The correct management and the best act of life depend on the stage of knowledge gain through circumstance which that life has faced. And knowledge gain determines the weight of that experience acts.

In life, hardship opens many ways and enlightens the mind for good planning, and life progress through the weight of the lessons solved. Every human being needs experience in life in order to act well; else the life will be abused by circumstance.

The youth need more to learn about life and be able to behave well. Their age needs many lessons and their parents must teach them about life matters to guide them for better stage management.

15. The effect of every Deed

Life is about actions and the result is the fruit that bears. The waves of the sea speak a lot and bear the witness of acts. Our first parents have brought deep damage to us through their acts.

Our hope shakes every day as the result acts. The testimony of every person stands on his or her actions.

Every act carries all the answers equal to the stage of that life and there is no witness that carries the weight than our acts.

Our life progress by the response to the laws governs nature and the acts are the advocate of a true witness who decides our stand whether to the left or right.

The youth must observe their acts seriously and be careful of their movement. The world we live has two options and the options have the reward which no one can escape.

It is definite result of which we cannot do way, and it will be a home for everyone who is privileged to live the world, and everyone possesses the one at the end whether like or not. Every act makes a home and that is the reward of that act.

Our acts identify the speech and the nature of that speech testifies the attitude of that person. Life acts impact a lot, and the result of that influence makes a home for us.

Let consider this scripture;

Mathew 18:7 Woe to the world because of the things that cause people to stumble! Such things must come, but woe to the person through whom they come!

People in the world have a lot to count, let's note that our actions are rocket bombs that destroy strong mountains and cause cracks to the earth and makes dust in the air for people to be affected.

Many of the youth acts cause damage and serious effect than they think. As the fire cause damage so as to the acts we intend; we should not take things for granted, all manners of life has the result and everything deeds on earth will be counted.

Today's acts can affect tomorrow's destiny and the manner by which it was acting can cause eternal lose whether for you and to the others.

We will be judged by our acts whether good or bad. (Ecclesiastes.12:14) whichever acts that cause someone to fall or make somebody short among his or her brethren will pay the penalty. Let consider this scripture again;

Mathew 18: 6 -10

6 "If anyone causes one of these little ones—those who believe in me—to stumble, it would be better for them to have a large millstone hung around their neck and to be drowned in the depths of the sea.

7 Woe to the world because of the things that cause people to stumble! Such things must come, but woe to the person through whom they come! 8 If your hand or your foot causes you to stumble, cut it off and throw it away. It is better for you to enter life maimed or crippled than to have two hands or two feet and be thrown into eternal fire. 9 And if your eye causes you to stumble, gouge it out and throw it away.

It is better for you to enter life with one eye than to have two eyes and be thrown into the fire of hell. 10 "See that you do not despise one of these little ones. For I tell you that their angels in heaven always see the face of my Father in heaven.

We are more than what we think or see ourselves, God loves us than we know and cherish our life. All of us as human beings are dear to God, no matter what our condition or state; we are very dear to Him (God) and it cause all His life as a ransom for our life as an individual.

We must be careful of our acts towards our brethren and act according to what the law claim from everyone. That is, we should act decently in all our societies. It is very serious to act negatively and make people fall by plan and think that is okay.

Woe to you who intend to do that! It is better not to be in the world than to cause one to fall by your act. There is no way to escape from it and take it free.

Actions cause harm than any atomic bomb and destroy both the actor and the listener. We are born to be respected and have that matches life; there shouldn't be discrimination among ourselves.

Everyone has what goes with life and that is okay to make the community whole. Never value yourself than the other and think that you are up to the standard than your colleagues.

This attitude or act makes way for unforgiving sin to have a seat of people life and many people do not know how sinful it is to value themselves than the other.

It is dangerous to exalt yourself and look down on others. Every act in human life proves the stage of that person who acted and defines the nature of that being. The youth must act to respect and to act as to stand before God (The Almighty) and fear about their actions.

We all need to consider our actions and prove beyond doubt about the way and the manner we act because it will judge us in due time.

Every word or act that proceeds out from any person has the effect which can cause damage or repairs the damage. And it is like the waves of the sea, it spread to the wide point of the wished end.

Men! We have a lot to deal with and to learn so many about life and it matters. The worlds we live is not there just like anything else that can be taking and go for free, but it is about counting and calculation for the correct answer and make the difference about what to choose and what not.

Every act count and the words explain the state of each being. Your acts witness about your true or falsehood and define your stage. Never deceive people by your sweet words and pretend like honey with all the sweets.

Further, many people deceive and act like lovers but not from the heart. Other people discriminate but pretend as devotees. All these acts cause damage to our fellow beings.

Note that, your actions can cause somebody's death or life. Your appearance can bear witness about your attitude and make room for you.

Our life on this earth today means nothing but our good attitude today can be meaningful on the next new earth.

All that is done on earth has the stand or position that bears the witness about the true or false motive behind the act and magnifies or decrease the beauty of it.

Every situation in human's life witness about the starting point, and direct that life goal, and makes the lessons that it must be studied for better experience gain.

Any act style, define the beauty or the ugly that holds the actor but the result makes the identity of that person who acted.

Actions speak louder than any blast that man can make on earth. And if you act on anyway, you sound like dynamite that destroys mountains. We must consider our acts in all manners of life and behave decorum.

In a time of trouble, we must know how to manage ourselves and note that, in all conditions of life test our inner being and show the kind of persons we are. In good times, know how to behave and bad times as well.

The deed we expose bears the total of our nature. That conduct takes shows the maturity of that performance. But the results of every act have the amount equal to the total weight that takes place.

In all manners of life, our acts will judge us. Never act without consideration; never eat without consideration, never dress as without mind, but be considerate in all the things about life and live humbly and get the best reward. This is about your life and not a joke!

16. Notes of Reflection

Life is about considerations and the lessons which everyone must note. Today can be yours, but tomorrow will be someone else.

Everything concerns life is about eternal joy or doom. Never make merry without good and proper self-examination. Take the life as yes or no principle, everything more than this is evil. Never demand what belongs to someone else or withheld his or her rights.

Make no difference among men or women on the basis of value the one than the other. Show respect to all people whether child; young or adult and cherish them as well.

Do not show partiality in age among men or women but consider every age as due respect. Be patient in all matters of life and be ready for good or bad.

Plan correctly about the things you do and do the unique thing currently in the system and get the correct responses from the people around you.

Be prudent and act decency. Make Practice on good things and be kind to all people. Be ready to stand for truth and never deceive by your act; appearance or tongue.

Be alert to help and at the same time work from the correct heart. Work hard but not to abuse yourself, do away laziness and keep your time as well. Make peace with all men and do your part to promote justice as well.

Buy the truth but don't sell, share with others about what you know is the best and never cover what will benefit others.

Give as a hobby but never hoard up what benefits others, share the little as well as the big. Be diligent about your work and search for other avenues that promote life to its best.

Welcome people with a good approach and share your joy and sorrow as well. Be creative and do the best one day at a time.

Be the servant to others in all the service to men but not as door mart. Work as a master but act as a servant and be humble in all your doings. Be gentle but not too gentle; be forceful as the law requires but not extending.

Life again consists of integrity; gentleness, forcefulness, preparation and good planning. We must be wise and at the same time as unwise depends on the condition not to cause damage to those who do not understand us.

Let's set a good approach in all manners of life to promote human equality and to avoid differences. Let us show true love to all people and fear God. Amen!

Note this scripture;

Micah 6: 8

8 He has shown you, O mortal, what is good.

And what does the LORD require of you? To act justly and to love

mercy and to walk humbly with your God. Amen!

For Good Living and Knowledge Gain!
B. B. S. LIFE BOOKS.

Also by Bernard Benson Sarfo

The Fact Among Facts (1st)
The Fact Among Facts

Standalone
The Youth Murderer
Be Original Not a Copy
The Christians Science or Scholarship
Precious than Paradise
Habit makes future
A shelter from storm and rain
The Science of Life
The Strongest Lion Knockback
The Perfect and Inspiring City
Above Hope, Faith and Love
The Hero's Brave Decisions
The Weakest Among Plants

About the Author

Bernard Benson Sarfo is an acquainted architectural designer and a motivational speaker.He is a gifted teacher who continues to motivate and encourage many.

Read more at https://www.amazon.com//author/bbslifebooks.

www.ingramcontent.com/pod-product-compliance
Lightning Source LLC
Chambersburg PA
CBHW021808150726

47989CB00004B/1836